MW00470486

Prayers
for
Eternal Life

Susan Tassone

Our Sunday Visitor Publishing Division
Our Sunday Visitor, Inc.
Huntington, Indiana 46750

Dedicated to Pope John Paul II, who taught us how to live and how to die

Nihil Obstat: Rev. Michael Heintz
Censor Librorum

Imprimatur: ✠ John M. D'Arcy
Bishop of Fort Wayne-South Bend
November 10, 2005

The *Nihil Obstat* and *Imprimatur* are official declarations that a book or pamphlet is free from doctrinal or moral error. It is not implied that those who have granted the *Nihil Obstat* and *Imprimatur* agree with the contents, opinions, or statements expressed.

Our Sunday Visitor Publishing Division
Our Sunday Visitor, Inc.
200 Noll Plaza
Huntington, IN 46750

ISBN-13: 978-1-59276-196-8
ISBN-10: 1-59276-196-8 (Inventory No. T247)
LCCN: 2005937542

Cover design by Rebecca J. Heaston
Interior design by Sherri L. Hoffman

PRINTED IN KOREA

Table of Contents

Introduction

*M*ore than one hundred fifty thousand people die each day worldwide — through natural disasters, accidents, sickness, wars, and sudden deaths. How many die unprepared? People die unprepared because they have not thought about the importance of praying for themselves, their loved ones, and their friends. We need to pray on a regular basis so that we are prepared for our eternal life. This book offers specific practices, devotions, and prayers to gain the grace of all graces: *to die in the state of grace with the reception of the last sacraments (Reconciliation, Anointing of the Sick, and Holy Communion).*

How does a person prepare for eternal life? It begins with forgiveness and the **Sacrament of Reconciliation**. There is a great need for reconciliation. However, we should not wait until the last hour to seek reconciliation with God and our neighbor. It should be done daily. The best way to prepare our soul for eternal life is with a constant attitude of forgiveness in our heart and actions. We are called to exercise patience in adversity, love of neighbor, assistance to those who are afflicted, and a sincere devotion to Our Lord and His Holy Mother — all in the spirit of unceasing prayer, and humility, which draws down grace upon us.

The **Anointing of the Sick** finds its biblical basis in the letter of St. James:

> Is any one among you suffering? Let him pray.... Is any among you sick? Let him call for the elders of the church, and let them pray over him, anointing him with oil in the name of the Lord; and the prayer of faith will save the sick man, and the Lord will raise him up; and if he has committed sin, he will be forgiven. Therefore confess your sins to one another, and pray for one another, that you may be healed. The prayer of a righteous man has great power in its effects. (James 5:13, 14-16)

Holy Communion is truly Bread from heaven. Our final Holy Communion is called Viaticum. It is "food for the journey" from this life to the next to reach God. It is the nourishment to bring strength and peace to souls in their last agony. When the body is failing, we look to Jesus, Who is eternal Life. "He who eats my flesh and drinks my blood has eternal life" (John 6:54). Jesus in the Eucharist is the fullness of love for the soul and for the body on earth and in heaven.

The sick and the dying do not suffer alone. Their membership in the Communion of Saints is one of special honor. Those who suffer are of special concern to the saints in glory and the poor souls in purgatory. The saints do not want the suffering to miss the rapture of the reward the blessed ones now enjoy. If we accept our suffering and offer it in union with Jesus' sufferings, we obtain great rewards in the hereafter. Throughout this book, there are brief Scripture quotations and the last words from saints and other holy ones, to provide the reader with comfort and strength.

The holy souls also are in fellowship with those who suffer on earth. The holy souls pray that those who suffer will be spared the pains of purgatory. The holy souls look to those suffering for a tiny share in the merit that earthly sufferings still garner, because the holy souls cannot gain merit for themselves. Through this sharing, the holy souls can be assisted, while we can improve our final disposition.

Pray for the dying. They become the holy souls! Mercy on the poor souls will bring us also the crowning mercy of a holy death. Bishop Fulton Sheen said, "As we enter heaven, we will see them, so many of them, coming towards us and thanking us. We will ask who they are, and they will say, 'A poor soul you prayed for in purgatory.'"

St. Joseph Cafasso explained that Our Lady comes to those who are devoted to her to help them on their deathbeds. The very edifying deaths of St. Aloysius, St. Stanislaus, St. John Berchmans, St.

Joseph Cafasso himself, and many other saints are witness to this. Let us do what Mary does. Let us help the dying as much as we can and visit them when we can. Let us pray for them. One of the greatest acts of love is the assistance of the dying.

Call on St. Joseph. If a soul expires in the arms of Jesus, Mary, and Joseph, it will remain for all eternity blissful in their embrace. The hour of death in the Office of the Saints is called the hour of birth. Prepare for your own death. Recite prayers for yourself and the dying that are directed toward God the Father, Jesus, the Holy Spirit, Our Lady, St. Joseph, and the saints. The *Catechism of the Catholic Church* states,

> The Church encourages us to prepare ourselves for the hour of our death. In the litany of the saints, for instance, she has us pray: "From a sudden death and unforeseen death, deliver us, O Lord" (*Roman Missal*, Litany of the Saints); to ask the Mother of God to intercede for us "at the hour of our death" in the *Hail Mary*; and to entrust ourselves to St. Joseph, the patron of a happy death. (CCC 1014)

Let us all work toward the goal of possession of God, union with Christ, union with His Holy Mother and St. Joseph, with the saints, and with those we love and cherish, for all eternity.

I.

Prayers to God, Our Father

*L*et us glorify God for creating us to know, love, serve, and possess Him for all eternity.

Prayer of Thanksgiving to God

Thanks be to God for His love and mercy,
Thanks be to God for His boundless grace,
Thanks be to God for the hearts that love us,
Thanks be to God for each friendly face.
Thanks be to God for strength in suffering,
Thanks be to God for joys we've known,
Thanks be to God for the hope He gives us,
of rest eternal beside His throne.

ST. JOHN EUDES

You will be with me in Paradise.
— LUKE 23:43

Covenant With God

O my God, Lover of the sick and the afflicted, being cast down on my bed of pain, I cannot pray as much as I desire. Accept each pain, each heartbeat, each tear, each sigh, as an act of love, of submission to Your Holy Will, and of sorrow for my sins.

My heart shall supply what my lips cannot do. Accept my good will for the dead, and let my suffering be pleasing in Your sight. Amen.

Prayer to the Holy Spirit

At the end of His earthly journey, Jesus petitioned the Father to send the Holy Spirit, our Advocate in both life and at the time of death.

Holy Spirit,
be present to all who are dying:
sustain them by Your power,
console them by Your love.

Even in their sufferings,
fill them with Your joy.

When their eyes
close to the things of this world,
grant that they may open them again on You,
unfailing Light.

And grant that, losing this world,
they may gain all things,
resting in the eternal possession of You. Amen.

I see my God. He calls me to Him.
— ST. ANTHONY OF PADUA

Act of Contrition

O my God, I am heartily sorry for having offended You, and I detest all my sins because of Your just punishments; but most of all because I have offended You, my God, who are all good and deserving of all my love. I firmly resolve, with the help of Your grace, to sin no more and to avoid the near occasion of sin. Amen.

Act of Faith

O my God, I firmly believe that You are one God in three divine Persons: Father, Son, and Holy Spirit. I believe that Your divine Son became man and died for our sins, and that He shall come to judge the living and the dead. I believe these and all the truths that the holy Catholic Church teaches, because You have revealed them, Who can neither deceive nor be deceived. Amen.

Act of Hope

O my God, relying on Your almighty power and infinite mercy and promises, I hope to obtain pardon for my sins, the help of Your grace, and life everlasting, through the merits of Jesus Christ, my Lord and Redeemer. Amen.

> *L et me go to the house of the Father.*
> — POPE JOHN PAUL II

Act of Love

O my God, I love You above all things, with my whole heart and soul, because You are all good and worthy of all love. I love my neighbor as myself for the love of You. I forgive all who have injured me and ask pardon of all whom I have injured. Amen.

Act of Adoration

With deepest humility, I adore You, my Lord and my God. You have made my soul Your dwelling place. I adore You as my Creator from Whose hand I came and with Whom I am to be happy forever. Amen.

Prayer for a Sick Person

(Note: "She" may be substituted for "he," and "her" for "him" and "his.")

O my God, behold this sick person before You. He has come to ask You what he wishes and what he considers as the most important thing for him. You, O my God, make these words enter in his heart: "*What is important is the health of my soul.*"

Lord, may Your will in everything be done in his regard. If You want him to be cured, let health be given to him; purify our hearts, to make us worthy to convey Your holy mercy.

Protect him and relieve his pain, that Your holy will be done in him, that Your Holy Name be revealed through him; help him bear his cross with courage.

Glory be … (three times)

Prayer for Daily Neglects

Eternal Father, I offer You the Sacred Heart of Jesus, with all its Love, all its Sufferings and all its Merits.

First, to expiate all the sins I have committed this day and during all my life. Glory be …

Second, to purify the good I have done badly this day and during all my life. Glory be …

Third, to supply for the good I ought to have done, and which I have neglected this day and during all my life. Glory be …

II.

Prayers to Jesus, Our Savior

*H*e died for us that we might live, and He lives for us that we might never die.

Act of Consecration to the Sacred Heart

O Sacred Heart of Jesus, filled with infinite love, broken by my ingratitude and pierced by my sins and yet loving me still: Accept the consecration that I make to You of all that I am and all that I have. Take every faculty of my body and soul, and draw me day by day nearer to Your sacred side, and there, as I can bear the lesson, teach me Your blessed ways. Amen.

Prayer to Jesus for a Good Death

Lord Jesus Christ, God of goodness and [mercy], I prostrate myself before You with a humble and contrite heart, and commend to You my last hour and what awaits me after it.

When my feet are deprived of movement and tell me that I am soon to be leaving this world, *merciful Jesus, have pity on me.*

When my hands are trembling and unable to hold the crucifix on which I look for comfort, *merciful Jesus, have pity on me.*

When my eyes are glazed at the prospect of death and fix their dying look upon You, *merciful Jesus, have pity on me.*

When my lips, cold and convulsed, pronounce for the last time Your adorable Name, *merciful Jesus, have pity on me.*

When my face, pale and livid, inspires pity on my relatives and friends standing around me or if I am alone, and my head is moist with the sweat of death, *merciful Jesus, have pity on me.*

When my ears, soon to be closed to the voices of men, are ready to hear from Your lips the sentence that will fix my lot for eternity, *merciful Jesus, have pity on me.*

When my heart, oppressed by suffering, is fearful of death and needs courage in its struggle for salvation, *merciful Jesus, have pity on me.*

When I shed my last tears, accept them, O Lord, as an act of reparation, that I may die as a victim of penance, and in that moment, *merciful Jesus, have pity on me.*

When I breathe my last sigh as the soul leaves the body, receive it, O Lord, as a sign of my eagerness to go to You, and then, *merciful Jesus, have pity on me.*

Lastly, when my soul appears before You and for the first time looks at the splendor of Your Majesty, do not reject me but deign to receive me in the bosom of Your mercy, that I may sing Your praises eternally. And then, and now, and always, *merciful Jesus, have pity on me.* Amen.

REMIGIO VILARINO, S.J.

Prayer to Avoid Purgatory

Most merciful Jesus, for Your dolorous Passion and for the love You bore me, I pray You to forgive me the punishments I have merited with my sins. Grant me, therefore, the spirit of penance, delicacy of conscience, avoidance of every deliberate venial sin, and the dispositions necessary to earn indulgences. I promise to offer suffrages as much as I can to the souls in purgatory; and, as soon as my soul is freed from the bonds of my body, do You, O infinite Goodness, admit it to the eternal vision and joy of heaven. Amen.

Our Father. Hail Mary. Eternal Rest.

Offering of Masses for the Dying

The Holy Mass is the summit of our faith. It is the highest form of worship and the highest act of prayer. We offer to God the greatest praise, the greatest glory. We make reparation and give Him most perfect thanks and adoration.

My God, I offer You all the Masses that are celebrated today throughout the whole world for sinners who are in their agony and who are to die this day. May the Precious Blood of Jesus, their Redeemer, obtain mercy for them. Amen.

Spiritual Communion

Spiritual Communion consists of an ardent desire to receive Jesus in the Most Holy Sacrament and in lovingly embracing Him as if we had actually received Him. Our Lord told Blessed Jane of the Cross that as often as she communicated spiritually she received a grace similar to that which she received from her Sacramental Communions. Make them frequently.

My Jesus, I believe that You are present in the Blessed Sacrament. I love You above everything, and I long for You in my soul. Since I cannot now receive You sacramentally, come at least spiritually into my heart. I embrace You and unite myself entirely to You; never permit me to be separated from You. Amen.

Offering Up Holy Communion as Viaticum (Last Communion)

My God, if I am to die this day, or suddenly at any time, I wish to receive this Communion as my Viaticum. I desire that my last food may be the Body and Blood of my Savior and Redeemer; my last words, "Jesus, Mary, and Joseph"; my last affection as an act of pure love of God, and of perfect contrition for my sins; my last consolation to die in Your holy grace and in Your holy love. Amen.

18

Prayers for the Dying

O Most Merciful Jesus, Lover of souls, we beseech You by the agony of Your Sacred Heart and the sorrows of Your Immaculate Mother, purify in Your Precious Blood all the sick and the sinners who are now in their last agony and who will die today. Jesus, our Redeemer, have mercy on them. Amen.

Agonizing Heart of Jesus, once in agony, have mercy on the dying. Amen.

Fear not, for I am with you.
— ISAIAH 41:10

Litany of the Most Precious Blood of Jesus

This litany clearly traces the line of salvation history through a series of biblical references and passages. Its present form was approved by Blessed John XXIII. The Precious Blood purifies our souls and raises us to a higher degree of holiness.

Lord, have mercy on us. **Lord, have mercy on us.**
Christ, have mercy on us. **Christ, have mercy on us.**
Lord, have mercy on us. **Lord, have mercy on us.**

Christic, hear us.   **Christ, hear us.**
                               Christ, graciously hear us.

God, the Father of heaven,   **Have mercy on us.**
God, the Son, Redeemer of the world . . .
God, the Holy Spirit . . .
Holy Trinity, One, God . . .

Blood of Christ, only-begotten Son of the eternal
    Father,   **Save us.**
Blood of Christ, Incarnate Word of God . . .
Blood of Christ, of the New and eternal
    Testament . . .
Blood of Christ, falling upon the earth in the
    Agony . . .
Blood of Christ, shed profusely in the Scourging . . .
Blood of Christ, flowing forth in the Crowning with
    Thorns . . .
Blood of Christ, poured out on the Cross . . .
Blood of Christ, price of our salvation . . .
Blood of Christ, without which there is no
    forgiveness . . .
Blood of Christ, Eucharistic drink and refreshment
    of souls . . .
Blood of Christ, river of mercy . . .
Blood of Christ, victor over demons . . .
Blood of Christ, courage of martyrs . . .
Blood of Christ, strength of confessors . . .
Blood of Christ, bringing forth virgins . . .

20

Blood of Christ, help of those in peril,   **Save us.**
Blood of Christ, relief of the burdened . . .
Blood of Christ, solace in sorrow . . .
Blood of Christ, hope of the penitent . . .
Blood of Christ, consolation of the dying . . .
Blood of Christ, peace and tenderness of hearts . . .
Blood of Christ, pledge of eternal life . . .
Blood of Christ, freeing souls from purgatory . . .
Blood of Christ, most worthy of all glory and
    honor . . .

Lamb of God, who takes away the sins of the world,
                              Spare us, O Lord.
Lamb of God, who takes away the sins of the world,
                        Graciously hear us, O Lord.
Lamb of God, who takes away the sins of the world,
                            Have mercy on us.

V. You have redeemed us, O Lord, in your Blood.
R. And made of us a kingdom for our God.

Let us pray: Almighty and eternal God, You have
appointed Your only-begotten Son the Redeemer of
the world, and willed to be appeased by His Blood.
Grant, we beg of You, that we may worthily adore
this price of our salvation, and through its power be
safeguarded from the evils of the present life, so that
we may rejoice in its fruits forever in heaven. Through
the same Christ our Lord. Amen.

Lord, into Thy hands, I commend my spirit. Jesus, Jesus!

— ST. ALOYSIUS GONZAGA

Let the Holy Name of Jesus be constantly invoked. The following prayers may be repeated to a dying person. Each time we say, "Jesus," we give God infinite joy and glory because we offer Him all the infinite merits of the Passion and Death of Jesus Christ. The Holy Name of Jesus saves us from evils and gives us strength, so our sufferings become lighter and easier to bear. We may also invoke God the Father, the Holy Spirit, the Blessed Mother, St. Joseph, and all of the angels and saints.

Jesus, Jesus, Jesus!

O Jesus, while I adore Your dying breath, I beseech You to receive mine.

Uncertain whether I shall have command of my senses when I leave this world, I offer You now my last agony and all the sorrows of my passing.

Since You are my God and my Savior, I give back my soul into Your hands.

Grant that the last beat of my heart may be an act of pure love for You. Amen.

— —

Holy Aspirations

- O God, be gracious to me; O God, have mercy on me; O God, forgive me my sins.
- O God the Father, have mercy on me.
- O Jesus, be gracious to me; O Holy Spirit, strengthen me.
- O God the Father, do not reject me; O Jesus, do not abandon me; O God the Holy Spirit, do not forsake me.
- O my God, into Your hands I commend my spirit; O Jesus, son of David, have mercy on me; O Jesus, son of Mary, have mercy on me.
- O Jesus, I believe in You; O Jesus, I trust in You; O Jesus, I hope in You; O Jesus, I love You.
- O Jesus, I place all my trust in Your bitter Passion.
- O Jesus, I hide myself in Your Sacred Wounds.
- O Jesus, I enclose myself in Your Sacred Heart.
- Holy Mary, Mother of God, assist me.
- Holy Mary, protect me from the evil spirit.
- Holy Mary, turn your eyes of mercy toward me.
- O Mary, Mother of mercy, obtain grace for me from your dear Son.

- O Mary, come to my aid in my anguish and need.
- O Mary, enclose me in your virginal heart.
- O Mary, commend me to your Son; present me to your Son; reconcile me with your Son.
- St. Joseph, assist me in my struggle.
- St. Joseph, to you I entrust my soul; save it for me.
- St. Joseph, remember me and obtain mercy for me.
- O holy Guardian Angel, do not abandon me, but combat for me and preserve me from the evil one.
- All you holy angels and saints, intercede for me and hasten to assist me.
- Into Your hands, O Lord, I commend my spirit.
- Sacred Heart of Jesus, strengthened in Your agony by an angel, strengthen us in our agony.
- Jesus, Mary, and Joseph, I love you; save souls.
- Mary, Mother of grace and Mother of mercy, protect us from our enemy and receive us at the hour of our death.
- In You, O Lord, I have hope; let me never be confounded.
- Hail, O Cross, you are my hope.
- My Jesus, mercy.
- My Jesus, I cling to You with my whole heart.
- Jesus, remember me when You come into Your kingdom.

Litany of the Most Holy Name of Jesus

This is an all-powerful prayer in honor of the Holy Name of Jesus. Have confidence in His Name.

Lord, have mercy on us.   **Lord, have mercy on us.**
Christ, have mercy on us. **Christ, have mercy on us**.
Lord, have mercy on us.   **Lord, have mercy on us.**
Christ, hear us.   **Christ, hear us.**
                    Christ, graciously hear us.

God, the Father of heaven,   **Have mercy on us.**
God, the Son, Redeemer of the world . . .
God, the Holy Spirit . . .
Holy Trinity, One God . . .

Jesus, Son of the living God,   **Have mercy on us.**
Jesus, splendor of the Father . . .
Jesus, brightness of eternal light . . .
Jesus, king of glory . . .
Jesus, sun of justice . . .
Jesus, Son of the Virgin Mary . . .
Jesus, most amiable . . .
Jesus, most admirable . . .

Jesus, the mighty God, **Have mercy on us.**
Jesus, father of the world to come ...
Jesus, angel of great counsel ...
Jesus, most powerful ...
Jesus, most patient ...
Jesus, most obedient ...
Jesus, meek and humble of heart ...
Jesus, lover of chastity ...
Jesus, our lover ...
Jesus, God of peace ...
Jesus, author of life ...
Jesus, model of virtues ...
Jesus, zealous for souls ...
Jesus, our God ...
Jesus, our refuge ...
Jesus, father of the poor ...
Jesus, treasure of the faithful ...
Jesus, Good Shepherd ...
Jesus, the true light ...
Jesus, eternal wisdom ...
Jesus, infinite goodness ...
Jesus, our way and our life ...
Jesus, joy of angels ...
Jesus, king of patriarchs ...
Jesus, master of the apostles ...
Jesus, teacher of the evangelists ...
Jesus, strength of martyrs ...
Jesus, light of confessors ...

Jesus, purity of virgins,   **Have mercy on us.**
Jesus, crown of all saints ...

Be merciful,   **Spare us, O Jesus.**
Be merciful,   **Graciously hear us, O Jesus.**

From all evil,   **Deliver us, O Jesus.**
From all sin ...
From Your wrath ...
From the snares of the devil ...
From the spirit of fornication ...
From everlasting death ...
From the neglect of Your inspirations ...
Through the mystery of Your Holy Incarnation ...
Through Your infancy ...
Through Your most divine life ...
Through Your labors ...
Through Your agony and Passion ...
Through Your cross and dereliction ...
Through your sufferings ...
Through Your death and burial ...
Through Your Resurrection ...
Through Your Ascension ...
Through Your institution of the Most Holy
    Eucharist ...
Through Your joys ...
Through Your glory ...

Lamb of God, Who takes away the sins of the
world,   **Have mercy on us, O Jesus.**
Lamb of God, Who takes away the sins of the
world,   **Have mercy on us, O Jesus.**
Lamb of God, Who takes away the sins of the
world,   **Have mercy on us, O Jesus.**

Jesus, hear us.   **Jesus, graciously hear us.**

Let us pray: Lord, may we who honor the Holy Name
of Jesus enjoy His friendship in this life, and be filled
with eternal joy in the kingdom where He lives and
reigns forever and ever. Amen.

The LORD is my light and salvation.
— PSALM 27:1

III.

Prayers to Mary, Our Mother

We often need someone "in our corner." No one is as close to the Father, Son, and Holy Spirit as Our Lady. When she speaks, the Trinity listens; not because they must, but because she is so irresistible. Our Lady, intercede for us!

The Rosary

Pray Our Lady's Rosary daily. Through the Rosary, we will save ourselves, we will console Our Lady and Our Lord, and we will obtain the salvation of many souls.

Act of Consecration to Mary Most Holy

O Mary, conceived without sin, pray for us who have recourse to thee. O Refuge of sinners, Mother of the dying, do not abandon us in the hour of our death, but obtain for us perfect sorrow, sincere contrition, remission of our sins, a worthy reception of the Most Holy Viaticum, and the strengthening help of the Sacrament of the Sick, that we may present ourselves with security before the throne of the just but merciful Judge, our God and Redeemer. Amen.

THE RACCOLTA

I have loved you with an everlasting love. — JEREMIAH 31:3

Consecrating the Last Three Hours of Our Life to the Most Holy Virgin

Prostrate at your feet, and humiliated by my sins, but full of confidence in you, O Mary, I beg you to accept the petition my heart is going to make. It is for my last moments, dear Mother. I ask for your protection and maternal love, so that in that decisive instant you will do all that your love can suggest in my behalf.

To you, O Mother of my soul, I consecrate *the last three hours of my life.*

Come to my side to receive my last breath, and when death has cut the thread of my days, tell Jesus, presenting to Him my soul: *"I love it!"* That word alone will be enough to procure for me the benediction of my God and the happiness of seeing you for all eternity.

I put my trust in you, my Mother, and know it will not be in vain.

O Mary! Pray for your child, and lead me to Jesus! Amen.

ILDEFONSO M. IZAGUIRRE, O.P.

Litany of Our Lady of Loreto

This litany to the Blessed Virgin Mary was composed during the Middle Ages. Its titles and invocations set before us Mary's exalted privileges, her holiness of life, her amiability and power, and her motherly spirit and queenly majesty. Invoke Our Lady often, to wrap yourself in her motherly mantle.

Lord, have mercy on us. **Lord, have mercy on us.**
Christ, have mercy on us. **Christ, have mercy on us.**
Lord, have mercy on us. **Lord, have mercy on us.**
Christ, hear us. **Christ, hear us.**
Christ, graciously hear us.

God, the Father of heaven, **Have mercy on us.**
God, the Son, Redeemer of the world ...
God, the Holy Spirit ...
Holy Trinity, One, God ...

Holy Mary, **Pray for us.**
Holy Mother of God ...
Holy Virgin of virgins ...
Mother of Christ ...
Mother of the Church ...
Mother of divine grace ...
Mother most pure ...
Mother most chaste ...
Mother inviolate ...

Mother undefiled,   **Pray for us.**
Mother immaculate ...
Mother most amiable ...
Mother most admirable ...
Mother of good counsel ...
Mother of our Creator ...
Mother of our Savior ...
Virgin most prudent ...
Virgin most venerable ...
Virgin most renowned ...
Virgin most powerful ...
Virgin most merciful ...
Virgin most faithful ...
Mirror of justice ...
Seat of wisdom ...
Cause of our joy ...
Spiritual vessel ...
Vessel of honor ...
Singular vessel of devotion ....
Mystical rose ...
Tower of David ...
Tower of ivory ...
House of gold ...
Ark of the covenant ...
Gate of heaven ...
Morning star ...
Health of the sick ...
Refuge of sinners ...
Comforter of the afflicted ...

Help of Christians, **Pray for us.**
Queen of angels . . .
Queen of patriarchs . . .
Queen of prophets . . .
Queen of apostles . . .
Queen of martyrs . . .
Queen of confessors . . .
Queen of virgins . . .
Queen of all saints . . .
Queen conceived without original sin . . . .
Queen assumed into heaven . . .
Queen of the most holy Rosary . . .
Queen of families . . .
Queen of peace . . .

Lamb of God, who takes away the sins of the world,
Spare us, O Lord.
Lamb of God, who takes away the sins of the world,
Graciously hear us, O Lord.
Lamb of God, who takes away the sins of the world,
Have mercy on us.

V. Pray for us, O holy Mother of God.
R. That we may be made worthy of the promises of Christ.

Let us pray: Grant, we beg You, O Lord God, that we, Your servants, may enjoy health of mind and body, and by the glorious intercession of the Blessed

Mother be delivered from present sorrow and enter into the joy of eternal happiness. Through Christ our Lord. Amen.

Holy Mary, Mother of God, pray for me a sinner, a poor sinner.

— ST. BERNADETTE SOUBIROUS

Memorare

Remember, O most gracious Virgin Mary, that never was it known that anyone who fled to thy protection, implored thy help, or sought thy intercession, was left unaided. Inspired by this confidence, I fly unto thee, O Virgin of virgins, my Mother. To thee do I come, before thee I stand, sinful and sorrowful. O Mother of the Word Incarnate, despise not my petitions, but in thy mercy hear and answer me. Amen.

To Our Lady, the Angels, and the Saints

O Mary, the most sweet Virgin Mother of our Lord,
    the most glorious Queen of Heaven, intercede
    for me with your Son.
O merciful protectress of the oppressed,
Support of the weak and infirm,

Refuge of afflicted sinners, look with eyes of pity on me.

By your intercession let my heart be inflamed with a most ardent love unto our Lord Jesus Christ.

O all you glorious angels and blessed saints, intercede for me.

O you blessed angel, appointed by God to be my sure guardian and most comfortable companion in this valley of tears, pray for me.

O you my most special patron, St. _____, intercede in my behalf unto Our Lord, that living according to your perfect rule and example I may with you contemplate His beautiful face. Amen.

ABBOT LOUIS DE BLOIS

O heaven, heaven. . . . What happiness! I am going to heaven. Do you not see that Lady over there? Oh, isn't she beautiful. Listen to the bells ringing. I see many little children dressed in white.
— SISTER CELINE (SISTER OF ST. THÉRÈSE OF LISIEUX, THE LITTLE FLOWER)

IV.

Prayers to St. Joseph, Our Patron

Go to Joseph! He is the patron of a happy death. He is the foster-father of our Savior. His power is dreadful to the devils. It has been said that his death was the most singularly privileged and the happiest ever experienced. He died in the arms of Jesus and Mary. May we, too, die in their embrace.

Prayers to the Holy Family

Grant unto us, O Lord Jesus, always to imitate the example of the Holy Family, so that in the hour of our death Your glorious Virgin Mother, together with blessed Joseph, may come to meet us, and that we may merit to be received by You into everlasting dwelling places. Who lives and reigns world without end. Amen. THE ROMAN BREVIARY

Jesus, Mary, and Joseph, I give you my heart and my soul.

Jesus, Mary, and Joseph, assist me in the hour of my death.

Jesus, Mary, and Joseph, may I die and rest in peace with you. Amen.

Jesu, Maria. — ST. PADRE PIO

Prayer to St. Joseph, Patron of the Dying

Eternal Father, by Your love for St. Joseph, whom you chose in preference to all men to represent You on earth, have mercy on us and on the dying.

Our Father. Hail Mary. Glory Be.

Eternal divine Son, by Your love for St. Joseph, who was Your faithful guardian on earth, have mercy on us and on the dying.

Our Father. Hail Mary. Glory Be.

Eternal divine Spirit, by Your love for Joseph, who so carefully watched over Mary, Your beloved spouse, have mercy on us and on the dying.

Our Father. Hail Mary. Glory Be.

Petitions to St. Joseph for Our Dying Moments

O glorious St. Joseph, whom I contemplate dying between Jesus and Mary, obtain for me, as well as for all those who are dear to me, the grace of leading a life like yours, so that like you, we may die the death of the just, assisted in our last struggle by our divine Savior and His most holy Mother.

O Joseph, holy patron of a good death, I take refuge at the foot of your altar, to implore you to aid me at the moment when the sovereign Judge will call me to appear in His presence. When my eyes shall be ready to close to the light of this world, when my tongue shall be able to repeat the names of Jesus and Mary only with difficulty, come to me — come to present my soul to God who wished to be as a son to you, and obtain that the sentence He shall pronounce over me may make me a partaker of the glory you enjoy in heaven. Amen.

O St. Joseph, foster-father of Jesus Christ, and true spouse of the Virgin Mary, pray for us and for the dying this day and night. Amen.

Prayer to St. Joseph for Those in Agony

O St. Joseph, protector of those in agony, take pity on those who at this very moment are engaged in their last combat. Take pity on my own soul when the hour of that combat shall come to me. Do not abandon me; in granting your assistance, show that you are my good father, and grant that my divine Savior may receive me with mercy into that dwelling where the elect enjoy a life that shall never end. Amen.

Litany to St. Joseph for the Dying

(Note: "Her" may be substituted for "him" and "his.")

Lord, have mercy on us.   **Lord, have mercy on us.**
Christ, have mercy on us. **Christ, have mercy on us.**

Lord, have mercy on us. **Lord, have mercy on us.**
Christ, hear us. **Christ, hear us.**
Christ, graciously hear us.

God, the Father of heaven, **Have mercy on us.**
God, the Son, Redeemer of the world ...
God, the Holy Spirit ...
Holy Trinity, One, God ...

St. Joseph, foster-father of Christ, **We beseech you, hear us.**

St. Joseph, patron of the dying ...
Obtain for him forgiveness of sins ...
Obtain for him great patience ...
Obtain for him perfect resignation ...
Obtain for him a living and unshaken faith ...
Obtain for him a firm confidence ...
Obtain for him ardent charity ...
Avert from him the attacks of the enemy ...
Protect him from temptations that assail him ...
Preserve him from despondency and despair ...
Obtain for him the grace of Jesus Christ ...
Assist him and do not abandon him ...
Come to his aid in his weakness ...
Assist him in his abandonment ...
Obtain for him a happy death ...
Obtain for him a merciful judgment ...

Conduct his soul to the vision of Jesus, there to obtain mercy for him. Amen.

V.

Prayers to the Saints, Our Friends

$\mathcal{T}$he saints tell us that if we patiently bear our sufferings we will merit the crown of martyrdom.

Chaplet of Divine Mercy

"Even if a sinner were most hardened, if only once he will recite this chaplet, he will obtain grace from My infinite mercy. Encourage souls to say the chaplet which I have given you.... When they say this chaplet in the presence of the dying, I will stand between My Father and the dying person, not as the just Judge but as the merciful Savior."

— Our Lord to St. Faustina

- This devotion is recited using ordinary Rosary beads.
- Begin with one Our Father, one Hail Mary, and the Apostles' Creed.
- Then, on the large bead before each decade, pray these words:

  Eternal Father, I offer You the Body and Blood, Soul and Divinity of Your dearly beloved Son, Our Lord Jesus Christ, in atonement for our sins and those of the whole world.

- On the small beads of each decade, pray the following words:

  For the sake of His sorrowful Passion, have mercy on us and on the whole world.

- In conclusion, pray these words three times:

Holy God, Holy Mighty One, Holy Immortal One, have mercy on us and on the whole world.

Prayer to St. Benedict

St. Benedict gave St. Gertrude the following assurance: "All who invoke me, remembering the glorious death which God honored me, shall be assisted by me at their death with such fidelity, that I will place myself where I see the enemy most disposed to attack. Thus being fortified by my presence, they will escape the snares which he lays for them, and depart happily and peacefully to the enjoyment of eternal beatitude."

O holy Father, St. Benedict, blessed by God both in grace and in name, who, while standing in prayer with your hands raised to heaven, did most happily yield your most angelic spirit into the hand of your Creator; and has promised zealously to defend against all the snares of the enemy, in the last struggle of death, those who should daily remind you of your glorious departure and heavenly joys: Protect me, I beseech you, O glorious Father St. Benedict, this day and every day by your holy blessing, that I may never be separated from our Blessed Lord, from the society of yourself, and of all the blessed. Through Christ our Lord. Amen.

Short Prayers of St. Gregory on Our Lord's Passion

O Lord Jesus Christ! I adore You hanging on the cross, wearing on Your Head Your crown of thorns. Let Your cross, I pray, deliver me from the destroying angel. Amen.

Our Father. Hail Mary.

O Lord Jesus Christ! I adore You wounded on the cross, given gall and vinegar to drink. Let Your wounds, I pray, be medicine to my soul. Amen.

Our Father. Hail Mary.

O Lord Jesus Christ! I pray You by that bitterness of Your Passion which You endured at the hour of death, especially at the moment Your Most Holy Soul departed from Your blessed Body: Have mercy on my soul at its departure out of my body, and bring it to eternal life. Amen.

Our Father. Hail Mary.

O Lord Jesus Christ! I adore You laid in the sepulchre and embalmed with myrrh and spices. I pray that Your death may be my life. Amen.

Our Father. Hail Mary.

O Lord Jesus Christ! I adore You descending into hell, and delivering Your captives. I pray, suffer me not to enter therein. Amen.

Our Father. Hail Mary.

O Lord Jesus Christ! I adore You rising again from the dead, ascending into heaven, and sitting at the right hand of the Father. I pray that I may merit to follow You, there to be presented to You. Amen.

Our Father. Hail Mary.

O Lord Jesus Christ! Good Shepherd, preserve the just, justify sinners, have mercy on all the faithful, living and dead, and be favorable to me, a wretched and unworthy sinner. Amen.

Our Father. Hail Mary.

Our Lady! Little angels! Heart of Jesus! We go, we go. . . . To heaven, with Our Lord. . . . With Our Lady . . . and the Little Shepherds. — SISTER LUCIA OF FÁTIMA

Litany for the Dying

(Note: "Her" may be substituted for "him" and "his.")

Lord, have mercy on us.   **Lord, have mercy on us.**
Christ, have mercy on us.   **Christ, have mercy on us.**
Lord, have mercy on us.   **Lord, have mercy on us.**
Christ, hear us.   **Christ, hear us.**
                                    Christ, graciously hear us.

Holy Mary,   **Pray for him.**
All holy angels and archangels ...
Holy Abel ...
All choirs of the just ...
Holy Abraham ...
St. John the Baptist ...
St. Joseph ...
All holy patriarchs and prophets ...
St. Peter ...
St. Paul ...
St. Andrew ...
St. John ...
All holy apostles and evangelists ...
All holy disciples of Our Lord ...
All Holy Innocents ...
St. Stephen ...
St. Lawrence ...
All holy martyrs ...
St. Sylvester ...

St. Gregory, **Pray for him.**
St. Augustine ...
All holy bishops and confessors ...
St. Benedict ...
St. Dominic ...
St. Francis ...
St. Camillus ...
St. Nicholas of Tolentine ...
St. John of God ...
All holy monks and hermits ...
St. Mary Magdalene ...
St. Lucy ...
All holy virgins and widows ...

All holy saints of God, **Make intercession for him.**
Be merciful, **Spare him, O Lord!**

Be merciful, **Deliver him, O Lord!**
From Your anger ...
From an unhappy death ...
From the pains of hell ...
From all evil ...
From the power of the devil ...
By Your nativity ...
By Your death and burial ...
By Your glorious resurrection ...
By the grace of the Holy Spirit the Comforter ...
In the day of judgment ...

V. We sinners beseech You to hear us.
R. That You spare him. We beseech You to hear us.

Lord, have mercy on us.	**Lord, have mercy on us.**
Christ, have mercy on us.	**Christ, have mercy on us.**
Lord, have mercy on us.	**Lord, have mercy on us.**

Let us pray: God of mercy, God of goodness; O God, who, according to the multitude of Your mercies, forgives the sins of those who repent and graciously remits the guilt of their past offenses, mercifully regard this servant, N., and grant him a full discharge of all his sins, who earnestly begs it of You. Remove, O merciful Father, whatever is in him through human frailty, or by the snares of the enemy. Make him a true member of the Church, and let him partake of the fruit of Your redemption. Have compassion, Lord, on his tears, and admit him reconciliation with You, who has no hope but in You, through Christ our Lord. Amen.

> *The LORD is near to all who call upon him.* — PSALM 145:18

Recommendation to One's Guardian Angel for a Happy Hour of Death

My good Angel, I know not when or how I shall die. It is possible I may be carried off suddenly, and that before my last sigh I may be deprived of all intelligence. Yet how many things I would wish to say to God on the threshold of eternity. In the full freedom of my will today, I come to charge you to speak for me at that awesome moment. You will say to Him, then, O my good Angel:

- That I wish to die in the Roman Catholic Apostolic Church in which all the saints since Jesus Christ have died.
- That I ask the grace of sharing in the infinite merits of my Redeemer, and that I desire to die in pressing to my lips the cross that was bathed in His Blood!
- That I detest my sins because they displease Him, and that I pardon through love of Him all my enemies as I wish myself to be pardoned.
- That I die willingly because He orders it, and that I throw myself with confidence into His adorable Heart, awaiting all His mercy.
- That in my inexpressible desire to go to heaven I am disposed to suffer everything it may please His sovereign justice to inflict on me.

- That I love Him before all things, above all things, and for His own sake; that I wish and hope to love Him with the elect, His angels, and the Blessed Mother during all eternity.

Do not refuse, O my Angel, to be my interpreter with God, and to declare to Him that these are my sentiments and my will. Amen.

ST. CHARLES BORROMEO

O Most Precious Blood! O Jesus, O Mary.
— ST. CAMILLUS DE LELLIS

Litany of the Holy Guardian Angel

The angel to whom was entrusted the mission of watching over us is never nearer to us than when we are bending under the heavy cross of sickness. As a faithful and loving friend, he is ever present, to console us and enable us to benefit by our sufferings, and to protect us against the snares of the enemy.

Lord, have mercy on us. **Lord, have mercy on us.**
Christ, have mercy on us. **Christ, have mercy on us.**
Lord, have mercy on us. **Lord, have mercy on us.**
Christ, hear us. **Christ, hear us.**
Christ, graciously hear us.

51

God, the Father of heaven,   **Have mercy on us.**
God, the Son, Redeemer of the world . . .
God, the Holy Spirit . . .
Holy Trinity, One, God . . .

Holy Mary, Queen of Angels,   **Pray for us.**
Holy Angel, my guardian . . .
Holy Angel, my prince . . .
Holy Angel, my monitor . . .
Holy Angel, my counselor . . .
Holy Angel, my defender . . .
Holy Angel, my steward . . .
Holy Angel, my friend . . .
Holy Angel, my consoler . . .
Holy Angel, my patron . . .
Holy Angel, my teacher . . .
Holy Angel, my leader . . .
Holy Angel, my intercessor . . .
Holy Angel, my protector . . .
Holy Angel, my defender . . .
Holly Angel, my comforter . . .
Holy Angel, my brother . . .
Holy Angel, my preacher . . .
Holy Angel, my shepherd . . .
Holy Angel, my witness . . .
Holy Angel, my helper . . .
Holy Angel, my watcher . . .
Holy Angel, my negotiator . . .

Holy Angel, my conductor, **Pray for us.**
Holy Angel, my preserver . . .
Holy Angel, my instructor . . .
Holy Angel, my enlightener . . .

Holy Angel, guard and keep me.

From every sin, **Guard and preserve us.**
From every danger . . .
From every snare of the devil . . .
From every enemy, visible and invisible . . .
From pestilence, hunger, and war . . .
From sluggishness in the service of God . . .
From sadness and anxiety . . .
From hardness of heart . . .
From the unworthy reception of the Most Holy
    Body and Blood of the Lord . . .
From a sudden and unprovided death . . .
From the eternal death . . .

Lamb of God, who takes away the sins of the world,
    Spare us, O Lord.
Lamb of God, who takes away the sins of the world,
    Graciously hear us, O Lord.
Lamb of God, who takes away the sins of the world,
    Have mercy on us.

Let us pray: Almighty and eternal God, Who has cre-
ated me in Your image, though unworthy that I am,

and has assigned Your holy angel as my guardian, grant me, Your servant, that I may happily pass over the dangers of every evil, both of body and soul, and after the course of this life come to eternal joy. Through Christ our Lord. Amen.

St. Michael Prayer

St. Michael the Archangel, defend us in battle; be our defense against the wickedness and snares of the devil. May God rebuke him, we humbly pray; and do you, O Prince of the heavenly host, by the power of God, thrust into hell Satan and the other evil spirits who prowl about the world seeking the ruin of souls. Amen.

I adore the will of God in all that He decrees for me. — St. John Baptist de la Salle

VI.

Pious Practices to Prepare for Eternal Life

*L*et us prepare ourselves for the journey to heaven, our true home.

Recommended Practices
for Everyone

- Devotion to the Holy Eucharist: faithful attendance at Holy Mass and devout reception of Holy Communion
- Monthly confession and fasting
- Forgiveness of others
- Abandonment to God's holy will
- Visits to the Most Blessed Sacrament
- Daily reading of Sacred Scripture
- Daily examination of conscience
- Special devotion to Our Lady, including daily recitation of the Rosary
- Daily prayers for a good death (to live and die in the state of grace and to receive the last sacraments)
- Daily prayers for the dying, including the Stations of the Cross and novenas
- Consecration to the Sacred Heart of Jesus and the Immaculate Heart of Mary
- Devotion to the Divine Mercy
- Devotion to the holy souls in purgatory, including the offering of Masses for living and deceased loved ones
- Devotion to the angels and saints
- Devotion to the Seven Dolors of Our Lady
- Devotion to the Nine First Fridays (for the practice of this devotion, Our Lord promises

the grace of final repentance) and Five First
Saturdays (for the practice of this devotion,
Our Lady promises to assist at the hour of
death with the graces necessary for salvation)

When Someone Is Dying or Terminally Ill

Persons who are dying or terminally ill may offer their
sufferings for these or other intentions:

- Conversion of sinners (especially family members)
- Holy souls in purgatory
- Vocations to the priesthood and religious life
- World peace
- Success of missionary work
- Sanctification of the clergy
- Reparation for sins committed against the Blessed Sacrament and the Immaculate Heart of Mary
- End to abortion

Pray frequent acts of faith, hope, charity, and contrition, or say them for those too weak to do so for themselves. If possible, they should be wearing a scapular or scapular medal. Someone should be with them as much as possible, to pray for them, to draw their attention to God, Our Lady, and the saints by means of aspirations (short prayers from the heart). Impress them with holy thoughts of death, to trust in God's goodness and mercy. Remind them to be patient with their weakness.

Consecrate the sick and dying to the Sacred Hearts of Jesus and Mary. They are full of loving solicitude when the moment of death draws near, the precious moment in which their children will be born to a new and immortal life. Jesus and Mary look to us to help the dying in the soul's journey. They look to us to assist them to bring their children to birth into eternal life.

Follow these practices when death is near:

- Offer Masses for the dying person before death.
- If possible, call a priest when death approaches so the person can receive the Sacrament of Reconciliation, the Sacrament of the Sick, Holy Communion, and the Apostolic Pardon. (Read the Passion and Resurrection stories from the Gospels. Recite the Psalms, especially Psalms 23 and 51. Pray the Stations of the Cross. Recite prayers from this book.)
- Light candles and have holy water and a crucifix available. (Always keep a crucifix in the room.) Recite the Apostles' Creed.

- If a priest cannot be present, place the crucifix in the hands of the dying person; sprinkle him or her with holy water, and, kneeling, say the prayers recommended on pages 38 through 54. The Rosary and the litanies are especially important. One need not be present with the dying to pray for them.
- Even though the dying person appears unconscious, whisper the sweet Name of Jesus in his or her ear, repeat an Act of Contrition, and continue praying. The sense of hearing is the last sense to leave a dying person.
- When the person has died, place a small crucifix in his or her hands, and sprinkle the body with holy water.
- Remember the dead! They are dependent on our prayers. Offer Masses regularly.
- Arrange Gregorian Masses, which are thirty consecutive Masses offered for one deceased soul. Include these in your will. They can be offered through your local Missions Office, or contact Susan Tassone (c/o Our Sunday Visitor, 200 Noll Plaza, Huntington, IN 46750) for more information.

VII.

Sacramentals

*T*hrough His Church, God provides us with the graces that comfort and strengthen us.

Sacramentals are intended to be instruments of grace. Blessed salt, holy water, medals, and so on, sanctify us, not of themselves, but by power flowing from the redemptive act of Jesus, elicited by the Church's intercession to be directed through those external signs and elements. It is good to wear or carry these blessed objects and have them in your home and car.

Bible: Reading Scripture, either silently or aloud, can be a very powerful means of grace. The Psalms, in particular, provide a wide variety of prayers, including prayers of petition, praise, and comfort.

Blessed Candles: These are the oldest sacramentals in the Church. The wax represents the pure body of Christ. The wick represents the soul of Christ. The flame stands for His divinity and the true Light of the world. We are children of the light.

Blessed Oil: Used in the Sacrament of the Anointing of the Sick, it is a source of spiritual and physical healing.

Blessed Palms: These remind us of the victory won by Christ and of us triumphing over ourselves.

Blessed Salt: Sign of everlasting life and a means to drive away all evil spirits, it can be sprinkled around and under the sick bed.

Crucifix or St. Benedict Crucifix: Place one on the wall facing the dying person or use a handheld crucifix. The crucifix reminds us of Who suffered for us, what He suffered for us, and why He suffered for us.

Holy Water: Because of the blessing attached to it, the Church strongly urges its use upon Her children, especially when dangers threaten, such as fire, storms, sickness, discord, and other calamities. You can sprinkle it around the sick room as well.

Images: Images of Our Lord, Our Lady, St. Joseph, St. Michael, and favorite saints serve to inspire, instill devotion, and stir the soul when words fail.

Medals: These are designed to increase devotion and protect the soul and the body of the wearer. Popular medals include Miraculous, Holy Face, Sacred Heart Badge, St. Benedict, St. Jude, St. Michael, St. Joseph, Agnus Dei, and favorite saints.

Prayer Books: The Church has a rich heritage of prayer that has come down through the ages. Use prayers for others or for yourself. Keep prayer books on hand to use at home and to take for hospital or home visitations.

Relics: Veneration of relics brings you nearer to the saints and to God.

Rosary: This is the most powerful Marian prayer on earth, which reflects on the life of Christ and His Mother.

Scapulars: Scapulars (Brown, Green, Five-Fold, and so on) give wearers a share in the merits, prayers, and spiritual benefits of the group whose badge it is. Wear it if possible — or pin it on the person's garment, wrap it around the person's wrist or ankle, or leave it in the sick room.

Sick Room Altar: This is a small table covered with a white cloth, on which is placed a crucifix, a holy statue or picture (of the Sacred Heart, Our Lady, or a favorite saint), candles, and perhaps flowers or a plant. It provides comfort to the sick and echoes the inspiration of the liturgy of the Church.

> *No eye has seen, nor ear heard, nor the heart of man conceived, what God has prepared for those who love him.*
>
> — 1 Corinthians 2:9

Bibliography

Blossoms of the Cross, Emmy Giehrl (published by the Sisters of St. Joseph, Indianapolis; printed by Carlon & Hollenbeck: 1894).

Handmaid of the Divine Physician: The Religious Care of the Sick and Dying, Sister Mary Berenice (Beck), O.S.F., R.N., Ph.D. (Bruce Publishing Company, Milwaukee: 1952).

Happy Hours With Christ, Clara M. Tiry (Bruce Publishing Company, Milwaukee: 1940).

Life Everlasting: A Theological Treatise on the Last Four Things — Death, Judgment, Heaven, Hell, Rev. Reginald Garrigou-LaGrange, O.P. (TAN Books and Publishers, Inc., Rockford, Ill.: 1952).

Preparation for Death, St. Alphonsus Liguori (TAN Books and Publishers, Inc., Rockford, Ill.: 1982).

Talks on Sacramentals, Father Arthur Tonne (Didde Printing Co.: 1950).

Ten Blessed Years: The Apostolate of Suffering, 1926-1936, Clara M. Tiry (The Apostolate of Suffering, Milwaukee: 1959).

The Holy Trinity Book of Prayers, Rt. Rev. Msgr. John K. Ryan, Ph.D. (P. J. Kenedy & Sons, New York: 1952).

The Sick Call Ritual, Rev. James E. Greenan (The Macmillan Company, New York: 1926).